STEAM

Railways Around
The World

The morning train from Chama begins the ascent of the Cumbres Pass, USA.

June 1990

STEAM

Railways Around
The World

KEITH STRICKLAND

Foreword by Miles Kington

Acknowledgements

The quotation on page 111 is taken from *World of South American Steam*, R. Christian and K. Mills, 1974. That on page 54 is from an article by the late James Cameron which first appeared in the *Guardian* in 1975 and subsequently in *Cameron in the Guardian*, Hutchinson, 1985.

A Sutton Publishing Book

This edition published in 1998 by Wrens Park Publishing, an imprint of
W.J. Williams & Son Ltd

This book was first published in 1991 by
Alan Sutton Publishing Limited, an imprint of Sutton Publishing Limited
Phoenix Mill · Thrupp · Stroud · Gloucestershire · GL5 2BU

British Library Cataloguing in Publication Data
A catalogue record for this book is available from the British Library.

ISBN 0905 778 103

Typeset in Baskervill 10/12pt.
Typesetting and origination by
Sutton Publishing Limited.
Printed in Great Britain by
WBC Limited, Bridgend, Mid-Glamorgan.

CONTENTS

A fortified station at Hangu, Pakistan, on what was once the north-west frontier of Britain's Indian Empire.

February 1988

The first train of the day leaves St Valéry on the *Chemin de Fer de la Baie de Somme*, France.

July 1984

FOREWORD

Somewhere in this book, appended to a photograph of a Peruvian station, is a prayer of thanksgiving by Keith Strickland that there are still places in this world where steam is such an everyday affair that nobody gives it a second thought. A true steam fan is not content with just finding steam engines in action, which is fairly easy to achieve at a preserved level or along tourist lines; he dreams of discovering forgotten corners where steam is normal, at a pre-preservation stage.

What he wants to do is travel back in time, to roll up the carpet of history till you get to the golden days of the 1950s and beyond when, as Keith remembers, it was possible to lie awake all night near Taunton and hear the engines clanking up and down. Odd how we can all remember the moment when we were infected by the disease of steam and pin it down much better than we can ever describe our symptoms to the doctor. . . . What Keith has been trying to do for the last heaven knows how long is not exactly to recapture his childhood (nobody ever admits to doing that), but to go in search of some magical music once heard long ago and still there to be heard if you look hard enough, because nothing since has ever sounded quite so good.

Keith Strickland is not alone. There are hundreds of steam enthusiasts dotted throughout the globe doing the same thing – pursuing rumours of an unspoilt steam line on a sugar estate in India, finding a branch line in Vietnam still using old Baldwins, or just goggling at the processions of steam in China. There are thousands of them standing in fields beside the line every time a steam special goes up from Settle to Carlisle, steadying tripods, sweating for the right moment, racing for the car when it's taken to speed on to the next spot. If just half of them turned their video records or their black and white albums into films and books, the shelves of the world could not take them.

Luckily, they don't. The videos get shown to friends and the photographs get shown to anyone willing to see them again. Only very rarely does someone like Keith Strickland have the determination and sheer obstinacy to battle his way into print. I'm glad he did. His portfolio of photographs is spread far enough around the world to make all but the most adventurous gricer jealous, and it captures the lump-in-the-throat, larger-than-life quality which only the steam world can conjure up. (Why is it that a steam engine always seems twice as big as any other kind of engine of the same size?)

I think it does more than that, though. His captions drop lots of hints about the places he has been to, and set the trains in their human context. For someone like me, who has a secret phobia of the kind of caption which describes engines as 'mounting an assault on an incline' or 'battling its way up the redoubtable . . .', it comes as a wonderful relief to have captions which tell you about the long lunches taken by French steam specials, or indeed the origin of the metre. (Did you know that the French divided the distance between the Pole and the Equator into two, and called each five thousand kilometres? I didn't.) It makes a difference, too, to be told that near a certain spot in China where he had been photographing trains he found the torso of a dead child, a victim of still practised infanticide. It makes a difference to find his own preferences come out in the open, as when he admits that he far prefers the bustling, steaming variety of India to the drab conformity of China. I couldn't agree more. China is far starker than anyone ever leads you to believe, and a lot colder too – and its trains are the dirtiest, most polluted I have ever seen in the world.

How Keith Strickland manages to combine this world-combing with a responsible job in Wiltshire, about which he is suitably vague, is beyond me, but it is probably something to do with the wife who actually appears in one photograph, set in France, which proves that some train enthusiasts are not always deserting their wives. I have always maintained that every railway fanatic has one book inside him or her, and that he or she very rarely gives birth to it. What I have never discovered is what happens *after* you have produced the book you've got tucked away inside you. Do you curl up and grow old? Do you transfer your affection to diesels? Do you set off immediately to chase your second book? I shall keep a keen eye on Keith Strickland to find out what really happens – meanwhile, here is a book that any railperson would be proud to have their name on. Some of these pictures are quite stunning. They are all very good. I might almost go out and get a camera myself, if I hadn't seen all those people in a field by the Settle–Carlisle line.

MILES KINGTON

PS I can answer one of Keith Strickland's questions. He asks, about a French locomotive, what all those outside pipes and devices can possibly be for. Surely it must be a dry run for the Pompidou Centre. . . .

'Pacific' 231–G–558 at Noyelles, France

May 1988

INTRODUCTION

Since 1974, I have had the good fortune to travel extensively in search of steam. At the last count, my collection of photographs covered twenty-eight countries, but until now, it has never seen the light of day except for an occasional picture in a magazine.

In discarding my modesty, I have only one aim. The photographs in this book are some of those which have given me particular pleasure – in their execution, in the end product, or in the story behind them. I hope they will give equal enjoyment to the reader.

A word of warning: this is not a technical book. My interest is not in boiler pressures, piston strokes or wheel diameters. Neither is it solely about steam engines. In some of the pictures there is not a loco to be seen! My love is for the general atmosphere associated with steam railways, and for the pleasure of trains as a means of travel and as a way of meeting people and experiencing places. It is this I have tried to convey. However, I have quoted engine numbers if known, and, where I felt it to be of particular interest, the class of locomotive, date of construction or wheel arrangement. Any errors are mine!

For those who like to know such things, all the photographs in this selection were taken on a Pentax Spotmatic F 35mm SLR camera bought secondhand in 1981. My preferred black and white film is Ilford XP1, and I normally use Ilfospeed paper in the darkroom.

Finally a vote of thanks to my wife. How have you put up with this hobby of mine for so long?

KEITH V. STRICKLAND
March 1991

Evening Star raises steam before her day's work on the West Somerset Railway, Minehead, England.

Easter Sunday 1989

ENGLAND

To begin at the beginning. . . . My childhood spanned the 1950s, the last full decade of steam on British Railways. To most boys of my generation, train spotting was as natural as playing games in the street. Encouragement came from my father. An early memory is of being sat on the crossbar of his bicycle to be taken to watch the trains. Mine wasn't really a railway family, though an uncle worked in the local permanent-way department, and a great uncle had begun a career as a messenger boy with the Great Western Railway on the weekend that the broad gauge was finally abolished in 1892.

Home was Taunton, the county town of Somerset and an important station on the former GWR line to the West Country. Seven routes converged there – from Bristol, Westbury, Yeovil, Chard, Exeter, Barnstaple and Minehead. It was a thoroughly Western place. The only foreign locos were the occasional Southern visitor from Barnstaple and a passing BR Standard or two.

Throughout my early train-spotting days, I was too young to appreciate the art of photography. Apart from a few blurred snapshots at the tail end, I've no visual record of the 1950s. Fortunately, many of the classes of loco seen at Taunton in those days can be photographed on preserved lines in England or hauling special trains on British Rail.

2–6–2 tanks handled much of the traffic on the branches radiating from Taunton. That to Minehead was the busiest, especially in the summer when there were through trains from London and the Midlands. After closure by BR in 1971, the line was rescued and now flourishes as the West Somerset Railway. As a child, I remember the beautiful countryside, the long waits at peaceful wayside stations and the Bank Holiday crowds. Happily, all these experiences are still with us.

5572 stands outside Minehead shed, while on loan from the Great Western Society's museum at Didcot.

August 1987

5164 is an example of the larger version of 2–6–2 tank engine built by the GWR, seen leaving Bridgnorth with a train for Bewdley, on the Severn Valley Railway. There isn't much evidence in this picture to show that it was taken thirty-five years after the railways of Britain were nationalized. The scene is so thoroughly Great Western down to the engine, coaches, signals and even the milepost, marking $149\frac{1}{2}$ miles from London (Paddington).

March 1983

Taunton was one of those places, now difficult to find anywhere in the world, where the sound of steam locos shunting could be heard all night. On still summer evenings, I only pretended to sleep as I listened to engines at work in the freight yards. How the imagination used to run riot, especially after the never-to-be-forgotten day when a friendly driver gave me, at the age of six, my first footplate ride in a quiet corner of a yard. This was on an 0–6–0 pannier tank, the like of which could be found all over the former Great Western network. 3738 now lives at the Great Western Society's museum where the atmosphere of a wayside country station is recreated at Didcot Halt.

October 1987

Today, when rail freight moves in bulk loads at express speeds, it isn't easy to remember the pick-up goods train slowly clanking its way from station to station, collecting the odd wagon here and shedding another there. From time to time some of the preserved railways attempt to jog the memory by recreating the distinctive atmosphere of the branch-line freight.

During its 1988 gala week, the West Somerset Railway ran a daily goods from Minehead to Williton. 3205, displaying the correct headlamp code for a pick-up goods, pauses at Blue Anchor. This class of engine was often used on the Minehead branch in the 1950s but never in such a pristine condition. Mum and her children wait to catch a Minehead-bound passenger train.

September 1988

Taunton shed (code 83B) had an allocation of some sixty or seventy engines but usually nothing more glamorous than a 'Hall'. A curious ritual was enacted every New Year's Eve. At midnight, the whistles of all the locos on shed were sounded simultaneously for five minutes or so. The town was left in no doubt that the new year had arrived!

6960 *Raveningham Hall* is kept on the Severn Valley Railway. Sporting an 82A shedplate (Bristol Bath Road) and an express passenger headlamp code, she crosses the Victoria Bridge with a train from Bridgnorth to Kidderminster.

April 1987

The same bridge seen from the bank of the River Severn. 7812 *Erlestoke Manor* hauls a train in the opposite direction. 'Manors' were rare at Taunton, though common further west in Devon and Cornwall.

April 1982

Summer Saturdays at Taunton were very special for they brought a stream of holiday trains to and from the West Country. The main line westwards into Devon seemed to be worked to maximum capacity. Perhaps the local railwaymen were harassed; perhaps the passengers were angry at the frequent delays. We were too exhilarated to care!

Memories of those days are stirred by 5051 *Drysllwyn Castle* hard at work with a main-line steam special, near Llanvihangel on the line from Hereford to Newport.

October 1985

Though of GWR parentage, 7029 *Clun Castle* was actually built after Britain's railways were nationalized. She climbs towards Sapperton tunnel with a special train from Swindon to Gloucester.

May 1987

Today, railway enthusiasts will travel tens, even hundreds, of miles to see their favourite express passenger loco at work.

How different it was in the 1950s. 'Kings' and 'Castles' could be seen any day of the week. On the West Country route out of Paddington, the crack train was the 'Cornish Riviera' which in the 'Down' direction ran non-stop through Taunton just before 1 o'clock – very convenient for a schoolboy's lunch hour. This train was invariably hauled by a 'King'; and there was a special thrill if it was 'the one with the bell'. 6000 *King George V* hauls a Swindon to Gloucester train near Sapperton.

September 1985

Even ardent Great Western fans were occasionally bored and yearned for something different. Fortunately, variety in profusion could be found not too far away on the Somerset and Dorset line. There one could see Midland and Southern classes and, latterly, locos of BR standard design. I vividly recall my first visit to the S&D sheds at Bath, when I was twelve years old. The shed foreman was surprisingly friendly and gave me a guided tour. What a contrast to Taunton where young visitors were always given the order of the boot. I still have my train-spotter's books, from which it seems I never saw 75069 in the 1950s or '60s. Here she climbs the Golden Valley near Stroud with a Gloucester to Swindon special.

September 1985

92220 *Evening Star* was the last steam loco built for British Railways. In the early 1960s, she often worked on the S&D, and hauled the last 'Pines Express' over the route. Now part of the collection of historic locos in the custody of the National Railway Museum, she has from time to time been loaned to preserved lines. For the 1989 summer season, 92220 worked on the West Somerset Railway and proved a tremendous attraction to the travelling public. She sits outside Minehead shed early one morning alongside 0–6–0 pannier tank 6412 and S&D 2–8–0 53808. In BR days, Minehead was a sub-shed of Taunton; and *Evening Star* carries the Taunton shedcode 83B.

August 1989

53808 is one of a class of eleven engines constructed specially for the hilly nature of the S&D. Though intended for freight working, they were often used in the 1950s to haul passenger trains, especially when traffic was heavy on summer Saturdays. Saved from the scrap-heap, 53808 was restored by the Somerset and Dorset Railway Trust, a process which took many years culminating in the loco's triumphant return to steam in 1987. It is kept on the West Somerset Railway where it looks quite at home – many stretches of the S&D were of single track. 53808 nears Crowcombe with a train from Minehead to Bishop's Lydeard.

August 1989

Bristol (Temple Meads) was another childhood haunt. A half-fare cheap day return ticket from Taunton cost 3/3d. (16p) in 1959. Ex-LMS locos on the line from Birmingham were the attraction. The 'Jubilee' 4–6–0s were favourites – after all, they had been designed by a former Great Western man! *Leander* is another preserved engine which has worked on a number of today's private railways. She is seen leaving Bridgnorth on the Severn Valley Railway.

May 1986

As a boy, I never really wanted to be an engine driver. I liked the thrill of the footplate but it seemed a very hot and dirty place to work. Signal-boxes appeared much more attractive. Maybe it was the sense of power which appealed! More likely it was the orderly atmosphere.

Radstock North Box originally stood on the Bristol to Frome line. After closure by BR, it was acquired by the Great Western Society and re-erected at the Didcot museum.

October 1987

FRANCE

My interest in steam worldwide began in the early '70s with the chance discovery of the book *Adieu dampflok*, a collection of photographs of steam on the continent by Jean-Michel Hartmann. It suddenly dawned that steam locos were still in everyday use on the other side of the Channel. The chase was on!

Chronologically, France wasn't the first country I visited. In fact by the time I got there, the national railways (SNCF, or *Société Nationale des Chemins de Fer Français*) had finished with steam. But the French preservation movement is flourishing, though not to the same extent as in the UK.

Main-line specials don't run that frequently and are often arranged at short notice. They have an ambience of their own – very French, and very different from specials in Britain. For a start, the trains are not run solely for enthusiasts, but rather as a day out for the whole family. Then, being France, lunch is very important. There may be a three hours' stopover; or a *Wagon-lits* restaurant car may be included in the train. Everything looks peculiar to English eyes: the low platforms, the functional appearance of locomotives, and the distinctive goggles worn by footplate crew. At least French trains keep to the left-hand tracks – a relic of the days when the first railways were designed and built by Brits.

Built by the North British Locomotive Company in Glasgow in 1916, 140–C–231 carefully eases on to the turntable at Longueville. The plate on the smoke-box door bears the initials AJECTA, the preservation society which owns the loco. The timber semi-circular roundhouse is home to the society's collection of engines at this depot some 60 miles south-east of Paris. 140 is French nomenclature for 2–8–0.

August 1984

140–C–231 in full cry at Chevrières with a special from Paris to Compiègne.

April 1987

'Pacific' 231–G–558 was constructed in 1922 and rebuilt fourteen years later, subsequently spending most of her working life on the Paris to Cherbourg route. After withdrawal by SNCF, a group of railwaymen bought the loco and set about her restoration. The French are not noted for a sentimental attachment to old objects, so it was to the new owners' credit that in 1984 they persuaded the government to designate the engine a *monument historique*, thereby obtaining financial support from the State.

The loco's second public appearance was at the head of a special from Paris to Rouen via Evreux, seen here at Boisset (Eure). There was great interest in this event. I met photographers from Germany, Holland and Belgium, as well as France and England.

October 1986

Later that day, the 'Pacific' was serviced at Sotteville depot, in the suburbs of Rouen. It is good to see that in the age of diesels and electrics, steam has not lost its magic for one boy.

Look at all that ironmongery atop and astride the boiler! What is it for?

October 1986

The railwaymen who own 231–G–558, during the course of a run from Caen to Rouen. They were not all on the footplate at the same time! The odd man out is the train's SNCF guard.

April 1987

After working a train from Paris to Noyelles, the 'Pacific' gets a rub down.

May 1988

France once had an extensive network of minor railways, *secondaires*, criss-crossing the country. Built primarily to serve the needs of local communities, many were of narrow gauge. Most found it impossible to compete against the motor car and bus, and few survived into the 1960s. Fortunately, some have received new leases of life in the preservation era.

The *Chemin de Fer du Vivarais* (CFV) operated 126 miles of metre gauge line on the eastern side of the Cevennes mountains. Total closure came in 1968 but the 20-mile section from Tournon (on the banks of the Rhône) through the valley of the River Doux to Lamastre reopened in the following year under new management. Since then, it has thrived as a tourist attraction in its own right, for the train provides the best way of seeing the spectacular Doux gorge. There is also plenty of interest for the enthusiast. Not only does the CFV possess a fleet of Mallet tank locos, but it retains the delightful rural atmosphere of a French byway.

I wonder how many passengers notice this sign, just before the train reaches Lamastre. The French invented the metre by dividing the distance between the North Pole and the Equator by ten million.

August 1990

Though built in 1903, 403 looks as good as new as she waits to leave Tournon with the morning train to Lamastre. In common with all the railway's Mallets, she is an 0–6–6–0. I love those headlamps!

June 1987

413 is of later vintage, having been constructed for the CFV in 1932. She makes a boisterous departure from Boucieu-le-Roi bound for Lamastre.

August 1990

404 has just crossed the 45th parallel and in a few minutes will arrive at Lamastre. The timetable allows travellers a four-hour sojourn before the return journey. There is plenty of time for a leisurely lunch in a town which claims to be a gastronomic centre – where in France doesn't?

August 1990

Lamastre station – from the outside . . .

. . . and within.

June 1987

The peace of the valley is temporarily disturbed as 413 coasts by with the return train to Tournon.
It's late afternoon, but the temperature is still in the nineties.

August 1990

A remnant of another minor railway, the *Chemin de Fer de la Baie de Somme* (CFBS) operates trains over 14 miles of metre gauge in northern France. Its headquarters are at St Valéry, an ancient port on the estuary of the River Somme. It is said William the Conqueror sailed from the town, although other places on the Normandy coast also make the same claim. At Noyelles the CFBS shares station facilities with SNCF's main line from Paris to Boulogne and Calais. The railway is therefore easily accessible from England and has a small but devoted band of British supporters.

3714 *Beton-Bazoches* stands on the quay at St Valéry with a short passenger train. She was built in 1909 for a light railway in the *département* of Seine-et-Marne south-east of Paris. There is no front to the cab, not because yesterday's railwaymen were a hardy breed, but because the loco was actually designed for cab-first running.

May 1988

101, an 0–6–0 of 1904 vintage, is also a recent import to the CFBS. She originally worked in southern Brittany on the *Chemin de Fer du Morbihan*.

The centenary of the CFBS was celebrated in 1988 with a weekend of special events: exhibitions, speeches, a parade of William the Conqueror's soldiers (or was it sailors?), wine-tasting, and plenty of steam activity. What fun they were! 101 chuffs into Lanchères with the first train of the day. The village band was on board and entertained passengers at each station stop.

May 1988

Later the same day, 101 leaves St Valéry with a train for Noyelles. The passengers look as if lunch was a satisfactory affair!

This section of the line is mixed gauge, the standard gauge rails straddling the metre pair (see the photograph on page vi).

May 1988

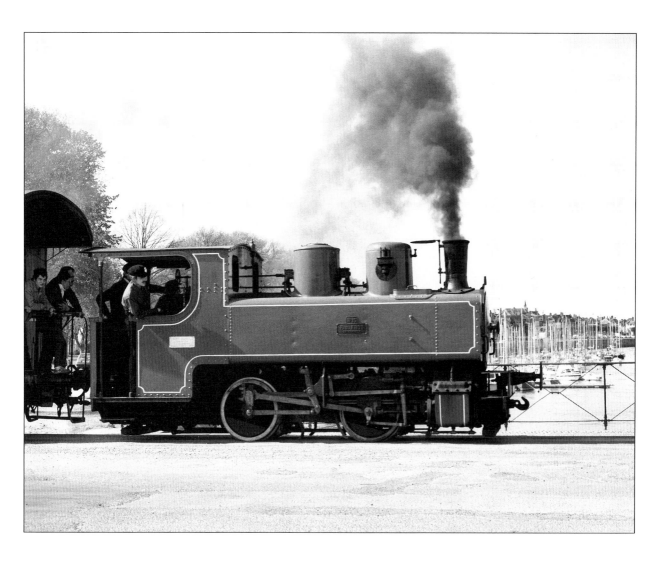

Engine 15 was built in 1925 for a public works contractor. Its diminutive size reflects its original use on temporary lines laid down in connection with large-scale construction projects. The loco was not intended to haul passenger trains and tends quickly to run out of steam. However, all is well as she crosses the River Somme on the outskirts of St Valéry.

May 1988

Pithiviers, a small town north-east of Orléans, was once the terminus of a 60 cm gauge roadside tramway to Toury. Passenger traffic ceased in 1951. Until closure in the mid-sixties, the line, which with branches once totalled 50 miles, was then used primarily to haul sugar-beet from the surrounding countryside to refineries at these two towns. Today, the station at Pithiviers is a museum, with a line four kilometres long to Bellebat – a run-round loop in the middle of fields. 12 is an 0–8–0 tank built in 1945.

The driver and my wife are doing their bit for the *entente cordiale*!

August 1987

GERMANY

Throughout the 1970s and '80s, the 'steamiest' countries in Europe were behind the Iron Curtain. Because railways were regarded in the same light as military installations, photography was often difficult, particularly in Poland, and sometimes impossible. Travel arrangements were liable to alteration without explanation. Most visiting railway enthusiasts went in organized groups on the 'safety in numbers' principle, but even this was no guarantee against official disruption.

East Germany was a different matter altogether. Excepting obvious military areas, there were no restrictions on travel or on railway photography. Hotels and visas could be pre-booked in the UK, and with the correct documentation one could take a car into the country. Furthermore, the Germans were used to seeing gricers as they have plenty of their own.

The Harz Mountains straddle the former boundary between the two halves of Germany. On the eastern side lie two metre gauge networks, the *Harzquerbahn* and the *Selketalbahn*. The two systems are linked giving a combined route in excess of 75 miles. In 1986 the lines were completely steam but diesels have since been introduced.

To cope with severe gradients, 1 in 30 being not uncommon, the *Harzquerbahn* had a fleet of massive 2–10–2 tanks, all but one built in the mid-fifties. 99.7240–7 prepares to do battle with the hills as she leaves Wernigerode with a train for Nordhausen.

May 1986

99.7234–0 picks her way through the outskirts of Wernigerode with another passenger train for Nordhausen.

Wernigerode is the northern terminus of the *Harzquerbahn* and location of the main shed and workshops. The central part of the town itself retains many attractive timbered houses: as the hotel barman said, 'Churchill didn't bomb Wernigerode. That's why we have so many old buildings.'

May 1986

One can't describe these locos as beautiful, but they were certainly powerful. To ride on the open balcony of the first coach was a thrilling experience, especially when the engine was working bunker-first, uphill on a wet rail. Pure magic! Ilfeld.

May 1986

99.7232–4 blasts out of Eisfelder Talmühle with a freight for Silberhütte.

May 1986

A train from Wernigerode approaches Eisfelder Talmühle. How long will scenes like this survive?
If private car ownership in what was formerly East Germany reaches the levels of the West, the
future of secondary lines must be in doubt.

May 1986

Eisfelder Talmühle. A station in the middle of nowhere. Here, a branch from Hasselfelde joins the main line from Wernigerode to Nordhausen.

On the far right, a train has just arrived off the branch; on the left, 99.7246–4 waits to leave with a passenger train for Nordhausen. She will be followed by the goods on the middle road.

May 1986

On the outskirts of Wernigerode, traffic is halted while 0–6–0 tank loco 99.6101–2 crosses the road with a short freight train from Hasserode. One imagines that today there are more western cars on the roads. Five years ago, the local product was predominant.

May 1986

On the *Selketalbahn*, sister engine 99.6102–0 leaves Gernrode with a train for Harzgerode.

May 1986

The *Harzquerbahn* and *Selketalbahn* are real everyday railways, though they operate in tourist areas and their pictures appear on local postcards. Both carry freight. On the latter, this is often as part of a mixed train. 99.6001–4 shunts wagons at Alexisbad in the course of working a mixed from Gernrode to Stiege.

May 1986

TURKEY

At one particular roundabout on Ankara's ring road there is a signpost which symbolizes the character of Turkey: one arm says 'Europe', the other 'Asia'. Turkey is a meeting place of cultures: Muslim and Christian, Oriental and Western.

Istanbul and the Mediterranean coast are on the tourist trail, but the remainder of Turkey is still only infrequently visited. It is not an easy country to get around, as the standard of roads is not good, and neither is the driving! Trains run hours late. Hotel accommodation is often best described as basic. Someone once said that Turkey was a good training ground for India!

Yet, railway enthusiasts have been going there for many years, attracted by the variety of steam locos to be found and the rugged scenery in which they operate.

By the 1980s, steam was on the way out, and confined to pockets of activity here and there. Long distances were involved in getting from one place to another, and much of the travelling was at night to leave the daylight hours free for photography. I remember arriving at a hotel at 4 a.m., stopping only for a wash, and checking out an hour later to catch the early light, despite the rain. My bemused host asked what was wrong with the hotel!

Turkey's engines originate from many countries, but the German influence is particularly strong. 46061 was the last of a class of eleven 2–8–2s built by the firm of Henschel, in 1937, for express passenger work. Working light-engine, she waits for the road at Pinarbasi, north of Konya.

April 1984

Lengthy stops at crossing-places are one of the reasons Turkish train journeys occupy so much time. 0–10–0 55013 sits for half an hour at Capali, near Karakuyu, waiting to pass a train in the opposite direction.

This class of loco dates from the 1920s and was built by German and Swedish firms.

April 1984

Turkey can be very hot in summer, and uncomfortably cold in winter. I was advised to go there in the spring. Sun? I hardly saw it in the wettest April the locals had known for some years.

Egridir was one of the master shots in the gricer's Turkish repertoire with a viaduct, lake and mountains. The viaduct actually crossed a dry gully but this didn't really matter. On the right day at the right time of year, the sun glistened on the water and sparkled on the snow-capped peaks.

None of this worked out for me with grey clouds the dominant feature. Still, at least there was a temporary halt to the rain. An unidentified 0–10–0 approaches the viaduct with the afternoon mixed from Egridir to Karakuyu.

April 1984

Another class of German origin, dating from before the First World War. 0–8–0 44043 ambles along near Gumusgun, bound for Isparta. On the only sunny day in a week's photography, the train is nicely framed by the blossoming trees.

April 1984

Part of the fascination of steam locos is being able to see the moving parts, even if one doesn't understand what they do. Two points about this photograph: firstly, the driving wheel makes one realize how small the flange is in proportion to the size of a loco, and yet it's the flange which keeps the whole thing on the rails; secondly, note the contrast in texture between the globules of oily dirt on the cylinder casing, and the smoothness of the piston.

The engine is an unidentified 0–8–0 at Burdur shed.

April 1984

The standard German 2–10–0 must be one of the most numerous types of steam loco built in Europe. After the Second World War, examples could be found in many countries where the German connection had been strong. This pair, 56520 and 56502, pause at Inay on the steeply-graded line from Alasehir to Usak.

April 1984

It's about fifty minutes after sunrise and someone doesn't look very happy to be at work at such an early hour. TCDD are the initials of the state railways – *Turkiye Cumhuriyeti Devlet Demiryollari* should you wish to know.

April 1984

An accident! The crane has toppled on to its side at Burdur shed, and there is quite a confab as to what to do.

April 1984

American superpower. Nearly ninety of these huge 2–10–0s (known as 'skyliners' because of the streamlined casing on top of the boiler) were delivered by the Vulcan Iron Works, Pennsylvania after the Second World War. 56357 edges out of Catalagzi shed into pouring rain.

April 1984

The station-master at Pinarbasi was very proud of his position, and of his children.

April 1984

I can't remember whether these happy children at Isparta station were waiting for a train or merely passing on their way home from school. One boy wasn't quite quick enough to get in the picture.

April 1984

And so to a British connection.

During the Second World War, twenty-five engines were shipped by the War Department to Turkey, though seven never arrived and lie somewhere at the bottom of the Mediterranean. They were built by the North British Locomotive Company in Glasgow in 1941/2 to the standard 2–8–0 design of the London Midland and Scottish Railway, the 8F. Despatched brand new to Turkey, local railwaymen there gave them the nickname 'Churchills'.

It had long been an ambition of mine to see a 'Churchill' at work. Relegated to shunting duties, not many were left in 1984, but 45161 was performing in the marshalling yards at Irmak.

April 1984

INDIA AND NEPAL

The late James Cameron writing in the *Guardian* once described India as 'a country so highly charged with its own emotions, so bizarre in its extremes of grace and wretchedness' as to impose 'all manner of jumpy responses from the Westerner'. How true. Is it possible to come to terms with the country in a rational way?

If there is an answer to this question, it lies in not judging India by western standards and through western eyes. By remembering this, the visitor can begin to relax, despite the poverty, the heat and dust, the crowds and their inquisitiveness, the bureaucracy, the power cuts, the mosquitoes and the stomach ailments! India exerts a fascination and a hold on many westerners, many of whom return again and again.

To see and experience the real India, away from the main tourist attractions, there is no better way than to take a long train journey. Railway stations themselves are a microcosm of Indian life: the homeless and beggars may spend their whole lives there cooking, eating, drinking, washing, living and sleeping on platforms or under the arches of bridges. Then there are people plying their trades – *chai-wallahs*, booksellers, stall-holders – and, of course, crowds. Indians don't arrive at the station just before the train is due to depart. They come hours, perhaps days, in advance.

At the end of the 1980s many long distance trains were hauled by diesel or electric locos, and some secondary routes had been 'modernized'. But steam could still be found in quantity on all three gauges: broad (5 ft 6 in), metre and narrow. On the former two, the variety of classes was much reduced. Even so, steam railways and Indian culture made an irresistible combination for many enthusiasts.

Something a little out of the ordinary. Delhi Rail Transport Museum has an 0–3–0 monorail loco in working order. Built in Germany in 1909, it was originally used in the State of Patiala. The large wheel on the outside stops the whole contraption falling sideways!

November 1985

Without doubt, the most distinctive locos on the broad gauge, from the point of view of appearance, were the WP 'Pacifics'. The first of the class was built by the Baldwin Locomotive Works in Philadelphia, USA in 1947. Twenty years later, the last emerged from India's own workshops at Chittaranjan. In all, 755 WPs were constructed. These were photographed at Lucknow.

November 1985

Another WP receives attention at Lucknow shed.

November 1985

Delhi Junction.

November 1985

Every visitor to India probably goes to Agra to see the Taj Mahal, and rightly so. No other building makes such an emotional impact. But Agra does not mean just the Taj. The Jama Marjid Mosque dominates the scene at one end of Agra Fort station.

1538 was a metre gauge 2–8–2 built by the American Locomotive Company, Schenectady in 1943.

November 1985

The standard post-war 'Pacific' on the metre gauge was class YP. Again, large numbers were constructed (871 in total) by British, German, American and Indian builders between 1949 and 1970. This one is at Varanasi.

November 1985

2337 was an Indian product, built by the Tata Engineering and Locomotive Company. She is pictured at Lucknow, a city well known to railway enthusiasts (with broad and metre gauge steam) but strangely not much visited by English tourists. The siege of the Residency during the Indian Mutiny was one of the most famous events in the history of the British Empire. The buildings were never repaired; and even today, the ruins are just as they were at the end of the siege. Prior to India's independence, Lucknow was the only place in the whole of the Empire where the Union Jack was not lowered at sunset. The flag was flown night and day in remembrance of the garrison's resistance.

November 1985

Another 'Pacific', this time on a gauge of 2 ft. Class NM was built by the English firm of Bagnall in 1931. 763 leaves Gwalior with a train for Bhind.

November 1985

The gentleman by the signal looked after a level crossing and kindly allowed me to sit in the shade offered by his hut. For two hours I waited. And then I contrived to make the tree grow out of the chimney!

760 heads out of Gwalior towards Sheopur Kalan.

November 1985

Every Indian passenger train has a number by which it is referred to in the timetable. Many long-distance expresses are named, and with what names! Whose imagination could fail to be stirred by such titles as the 'Assam Mail', 'Himalayan Queen' or 'Frontier Mail'?

Known simply as '675 Down', the humble 9.15 a.m. to Tantpur waits to leave Dhaulpur, headed by 707, a 2 ft 6in gauge 4–8–0.

November 1985

Train '674 Up' arrives at Dhaulpur from Sirmuttra.

November 1985

Without doubt, the premier attraction in India for railway enthusiasts is the 2 ft gauge Darjeeling Himalayan Railway. With the aid of loops and zigzags, this line climbs to a maximum height of 7,400 ft above sea-level. Progress is slow, as one might expect. 'Up' trains take eight hours to cover the 50 miles. But who cares? The scenery is superb, the diminutive locos are fascinating, and the sound of the engine blasting her way up the stiff gradient is music to the ears.

779 *Mountaineer* heads an 'Up' train at Tindharia about half way between New Jalpaiguri (the lower terminus) and Darjeeling. Built as long ago as 1892, she is in immaculate condition and sports a number of embellishments.

December 1985

Another shot of 779 at Tindharia. The job of the two men at the front is to sand the rails, the sand being kept in the container below the smoke-box door. With a driver, fireman and, often, someone to break the coal into small pieces, these little locos have a crew of five. It's just as well labour is cheap and plentiful in India.

December 1985

There aren't many private railways left in India. One of the few remaining in 1985 ran from Futwa to Islampur, though it has since closed. An 0–6–2 tank with the intriguing number IH heads a short train.

November 1985

All visitors to India are objects of attention, especially if pursuing unusual pastimes. Children are particularly attracted and materialize from nowhere. A crowd soon gathers, even in the most out-of-the-way places, as here at Islampur.

November 1985

Nepal is not the most obvious country for steam. Mention Nepal and most people think of Kathmandu and mountains. In fact, in the south of the country along its border with India lies the Terai, a low-lying fertile plain, flat, hot and mosquito-ridden. One of the border crossing-points was Jaynagar where the metre gauge of Indian Railways connected with a 2 ft 6 in gauge line running northwards to the Nepalese towns of Janakpur and Bizalpura.

This area is way off the tourist trail and wherever you start it's a long journey to get here. Moreover, the hotels in Janakpur are designed for the locals, not for westerners. But patience has its reward. Throughout the 1980s, the line was completely steam with a surprising variety of engines, including two Garratts. Of British extraction, *Mahabir* (built 1932) poses for the photographer near Janakpur with a special train. Did all the crew have a useful function, or were they there for the ride, or because they wanted their picture taken?

December 1985

Roof-top passengers are a common sight in India. They show not the slightest concern either for officialdom or for their own safety. These ride a train from Gwalior to Bhind.

November 1985

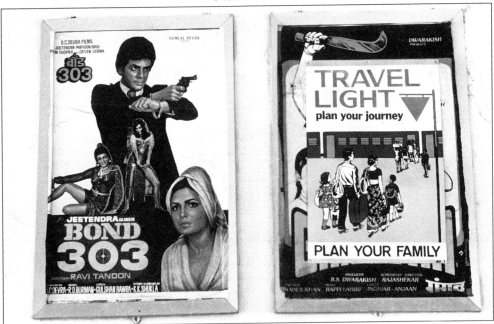

Every large station has its quota of film posters. At Jaipur, a different type of propaganda has been superimposed.

November 1985

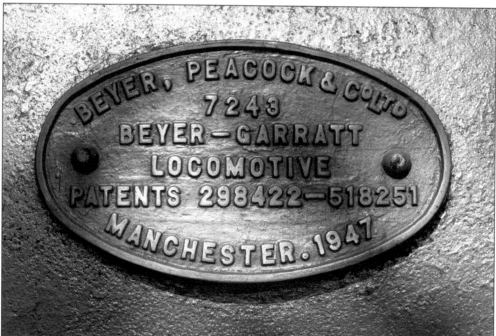

As might be expected, in the days of the Raj, Britain was a major supplier of locos. The top builder's plate belonged to loco IH of the Futwa–Islampur railway (see page 68). The Garratt loco was seen in Nepal.

November and December 1985

PAKISTAN

Since the British left the Indian subcontinent in 1947, India and Pakistan have developed in different ways with distinct cultures. India's constitution is secular; in Pakistan there is a close link between the State and religion. The population of India is predominantly Hindu; that of Pakistan, Muslim. This dichotomy manifests itself in a number of ways such as an absence of alcohol and the appearance of women completely dressed in black in Pakistan .

On the railways there are also distinctions. Pakistan's steam engines were converted to burn oil because, unlike India, the country had no coal reserves. India continued to construct its own steam locos through the 1960s. Pakistan's policy towards steam seemed to be 'make do and mend' so that most of its fleet was of pre-independence vintage.

Pakistan is not yet on the tourist trail. As a result, outside the main cities, western visitors often have difficulty finding suitable sleeping accommodation. One way round this problem is to sleep on the trains. In 1988, Railway Travel and Photography (RT&P), a Staffordshire-based travel company specializing in tours for rail buffs, chartered its own train for a ten-day journey to the remaining steam centres in Pakistan.

What an experience! The train was our home. We lived on it, slept on it, and ate in our very own restaurant car. Of course, there were problems. An absence of corridor connections between the coaches made access to the dining car difficult, and the most successful wash-and-brush-ups were under stand-pipes on station platforms or in barbers' shops in the local bazaars. But the difficulties were no more than a minor inconvenience and were more than compensated for by the pleasure of the journey.

The railways of the Indian subcontinent are one of the most obvious legacies of the Raj. The British parentage is evident in such features as signalling, loco design and operating practices. At the turn of the century, a body known as the British Engineering Standards Committee recommended the standardization of new locos for India. As a result, a number of basic classes evolved, one of which was the 2–8–0 HGS. 'HG' stood for heavy goods; 'S' for superheated. Locos of this class were built in the UK from 1913 to 1923. 2277 shunts the yards at Samasata Junction. Take away the headlight in front of the chimney, and she wouldn't have looked out of place in England sixty years ago.

This is a favourite picture because many of the elements which make up the atmosphere of steam on the sub-continent are here: heat, dust, passengers hanging on the outside of carriages, and even riding on the engine, bystanders, bicycles, signals, a venerable loco, and, of course, smoke!

Class SPS 2969 makes a noisy departure from Malakwal with a train for Lala Musa.

February 1988

A sister engine under repair at Kotri Junction shed.

February 1988

Among the British classes still at work in Pakistan in the 1980s, class SPS (Standard Passenger Superheated) was without doubt the doyen. In the history of steam locos, the inside cylinder 4–4–0 is one of the classic designs.

Many an enthusiast visited Pakistan just to see these engines, which were built in the period 1911 to 1922. The mecca of this pilgrimage and the home shed of the 4–4–0s was Malakwal on the secondary main line from Lala Musa to Shorkot. 3005 works hard *en route* to Malakwal.

February 1988

2964 backs into Malakwal station.

February 1988

This is a favourite picture because many of the elements which make up the atmosphere of steam on the subcontinent are here: heat, dust, passengers hanging on the outside of carriages, and even riding on the engine, bystanders, bicycles, signals, a venerable loco, and, of course, smoke!

Class SPS 2969 makes a noisy departure from Malakwal with a train for Lala Musa.

February 1988

The same train passing a mosque on the outskirts of Malakwal. The teacher kindly made sure his boys were sat neatly in the open-air classroom. Earlier he had provided tea and a discourse on the Pakistani education system as I had chanced to mention my wife was a teacher.

February 1988

Two 4–4–0s cross at Pakhowal. The approaching train looks rather full!

February 1988

2976 passes Malakwal West signal-box bound for Sargodha Junction. After coming out of school in mid-afternoon, the children here were a bit of a problem. Eager to practise their English, particularly on the topic of cricket, they swarmed around the unsuspecting visitor. When this happened, the signal-box became a place of refuge, thanks to an hospitable signalman.

February 1988

Another ubiquitous British design was the 0–6–0 tender loco. How many engines of this wheel arrangement were built in the UK for home and abroad? Thousands, one imagines. Pakistan Railways knew them as SGS (Standard Goods Superheated). 2487 has just come off shed at Malakwal. Look carefully as there are three more steam locos in this photograph.

February 1988

Two 0–6–0s struggle to lift the RT&P Special up the steep gradient of the Dandot branch. The leading engine is on the left, the banker on the right. Each has a tank wagon for extra water supplies. This was alleged to be the first time a restaurant car had been worked to Dandot, which normally only saw one train a day.

February 1988

Rawalpindi shed.

February 1988

From the old to the new. On the broad gauge, the most recently built class of steam engine was the CWD 2–8–2, constructed in Canada at the end of the Second World War. 5085 hauls a train from Bahawalnagar Junction to Fort Abbas.

February 1988

Like India, Pakistan saw steam on the broad, metre and narrow gauges. Metre gauge 2–8–2 734 passes a mosquito-ridden swamp *en route* from Mirpur Khas to Pithoro Junction. Freshly painted the previous day, the engine was embellished without . . .

. . . and within.

February 1988

The 2 ft 6 in gauge line from Kohat to Thal had one regular passenger train a week. A special from Kohat to Hangu is headed by 211, a 2–6–2 constructed by the English firm of Bagnall in 1933.

February 1988

211 not far from Kohat. This line was near the border with Afghanistan. Normally a flat wagon was propelled ahead of the loco so that in the event of a bomb on the track the wagon would take the force of the blast.

February 1988

Another narrow gauge line ran a hundred miles from Mari Indus to Tank with a branch from Laki
Marwat Junction to Bannu. Traffic was sparse but 203 finds some shunting to do at the junction,
where the so-called restaurant room displayed a curious notice: 'No talk of military matters here'.
I didn't find out the penalty for disobedience.

Spot the goatherds! There are three at work milking.

February 1988

The signal-box at Kotri Junction had a British feel to it. But I'd never before been in a box where birds nested inside under the beams!

February 1988

Men at work. Members of the RT&P party check cameras in preparation for a run-past near Kohat. The loco crew look totally bewildered.

February 1988

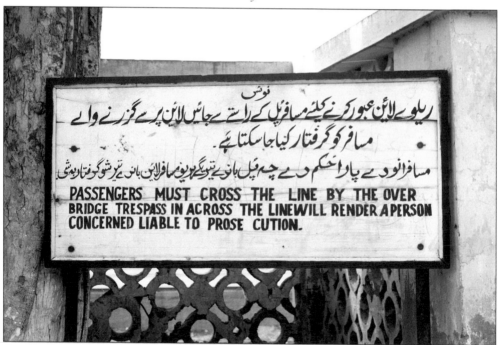

English as she is wrote at Kohat!

February 1988

CHINA

Communist China began to open its doors to western visitors in the 1970s. At that time, the handful of railway enthusiasts who were allowed in, found their travel severely restricted. They could only go where the authorities permitted, and often a silk farm or primary school was more likely to be on the approved itinerary than a railway station. But those pioneers brought back stories which hinted at untold numbers of steam locos. Then the discovery was made that steam engines were still being constructed in China. Suddenly, everyone wanted to go there!

Somehow, the realization didn't match the expectation. Yes, the Great Wall is impressive. Did you know, it is the only man-made feature on earth which can be detected with the naked eye from space? And there is nothing else quite like the terracotta army near Xian.

But despite its cultural heritage, China seemed drab and dull. Life wasn't as vibrant as in India and appeared colourless and regimented.

This uniformity was reflected in the railways. Put simply, though the number of steam locos could be counted in thousands, there wasn't much variety. A few standard classes were predominant.

On the plus side, both passenger and freight traffic were heavy. Many main lines carried a seemingly endless procession of trains. Railway operation was efficient with the punctual running of trains and well-maintained engines. Also, some incredibly long trips were possible behind steam. Where else in the world could I have made a continuous journey on steam-hauled service trains of nigh on a thousand miles?

The most common steam loco in China was the class QJ 2–10–2. Designed for heavy freight work but also found on secondary passenger turns, the QJs were still being constructed at Datong locomotive works in the 1980s, though production has since ceased. Chinese classes are identified by two characters (letters) from words with a political theme. Hence QJ derives from the Chinese for 'progress'. This member of the class rests at Feng-t'ai marshalling yards on the outskirts of Beijing.

November 1982

Datong is a centre of coal-mining and heavy industry. In 1982, the loco factory built over two hundred steam engines, employed eight thousand workers, and with its own housing, hospital and five schools, covered a vast area.

On the main line, two QJs prepare to double-head a heavy coal train out of Datong. This sight was repeated at fifteen minute intervals, so great was the volume of freight traffic.

November 1982

The Chinese are very proud of their engineering achievements. The bridge across the Yangtze River at Wuhan took from 1955 to 1957 to complete. It is a double-decker affair with road above, and rail below. An almost subterranean atmosphere is created as a QJ thunders across with a heavy freight.

December 1982

QJ 3070 hurries towards Datong. The board above the buffer beam displays the emblem of China Railways.

    This photograph has sad associations. Lying by the roadside not far away was the torso of a small child, evidence apparently of infanticide which still occasionally took place in remote country areas.

November 1982

A going-away shot of QJ 3070. I hope this picture conveys how bleak, cold and grey Datong could be in winter.

November 1982

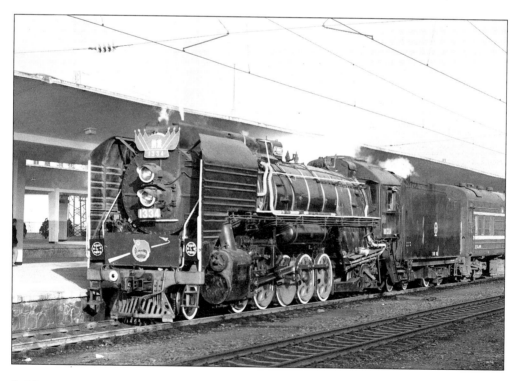

A QJ on passenger duty at Taiyuan.

November 1982

Xian was a very steamy place in 1982. Its shed had an allocation of 130 engines, and the station saw a hundred trains each day, every one steam-hauled. There wasn't a diesel or electric loco in sight. 1141 is a class RM 'Pacific' ('people's').

December 1982

One of the constant stream of freight trains passing Feng-t'ai marshalling yards, hauled by class JS ('construction') 5035.

November 1982

It is exciting to come across an engine with the number 1. The chances are actually good in China because a sequence of numbers is not unique to a particular class. This is an SY ('aim high') 2–8–2 at Taiyuan.

November 1982

There were, and probably still are, hundreds of steam locos at work in industrial locations in China. It is doubtful that all have been discovered. The steelworks at Wuhan alone had a rail network of 140 miles with fifty engines. As it slowly emerges from one of the mills, YJ 222 hardly lives up to its class title – 'leap forward'.

December 1982

Railway employees aboard a QJ at Badaling and looking after a level crossing near Datong. Near the latter was a dead dog which was unusual as most animals in China end up in the cooking pot! A proverb runs to the effect: 'If something moves but can't be eaten, it must be a bicycle'.

November 1982

Chinese children were intrigued as to why someone should stand for hours by an empty railway line in the cold wind.

November 1982

SOUTH AMERICA

I've unfortunately only been to South America once, and I nearly didn't get there then due to over-indulgence the evening prior to departure!

It's surprising that the subcontinent isn't a more popular destination. The variety of scenery and people is staggering. To the student of geography, South America comes close to paradise: lush equatorial forests, vast open plains, Mediterranean-type beaches, mountains, volcanoes, deserts, and so on. The contrasts are human as well as physical: shanty towns of the poor and villas of the idle rich, airliners and dirt roads, sumptuous food in five-star hotels, and chip omelettes from a roadside stall (the chips were *in* the omelette), wine from Chile to rival France, and Peru's own version of Coke – green Inca Cola!

My schedule was punishing: 4 countries, 10 flights, and 20,000 miles in three weeks. A holiday? Hardly. An adventure? Possibly. Exhilarating? Certainly. There were problems: the total closure of Brazil's petrol stations at weekends (which no one told us about!), tropical downpours, dreadful roads, no timetables as one train a day hardly justifies such an extravagance, and *en route* to the engine sheds, we experienced life in the shanty towns – railway buffs visit parts other tourists cannot reach. In Concepción (Chile), I had to lock myself *into* our hired car while the urchins climbed all over it to peer at the *gringo*. It was one of the few occasions I've wished I was somewhere else.

São João del Rei, Brazil is the headquarters of a 2 ft 6 in gauge system. Today it is no more than a tourist operation, but in 1981 it was an exciting 'real' railway, noted for its charming 4–4–0s, 4–6–0s and 2–8–0s built by the Baldwin Locomotive Company in the USA, the oldest as long ago as 1889. One of the 2–8–0s, 69, is being prepared for her day's work at São João. The rerailing jacks on the buffer beams were essential. On our journey, the front bogie was derailed when the train hit a mudslide.

November 1981

One of the last steam centres in Chile was Temuco, a town about four hundred miles south of
Santiago on the 5 ft 6 in gauge main line to Puerto Montt. An unidentified 2–6–0 shunts wagons at
Padre Las Casas prior to working a short freight to Temuco.

December 1981

In 1981, steam in Chile was on its last legs. In fact, the whole railway system didn't look too healthy. Starved of investment, the railways were finding it difficult to compete with road traffic. On the main line to Puerto Montt, just a handful of trains ran. In contrast, the parallel Pan-American highway saw a never-ending stream of long distance coaches all being driven at frightening speeds, and no expense was being spared to upgrade the road.

545, a 4–6–0 built in Glasgow by the North British Locomotive Company as long ago as 1908, heads a train from Tolten to Temuco. How did I manage to frame the train so neatly among the plethora of telegraph poles? Sheer luck.

December 1981

The same train earlier in its journey.

December 1981

The high point of the South American tour was Peru. It's many a year since steam was used on the well-known line from Lima to Huancayo whose summit is 3 miles up in the Andes. But the 3 ft gauge line from Huancayo to Huancavelica still saw steam in 1981 – just. The daily mixed alternated between diesel and steam. All other services were operated by railcars.

The railway's most modern loco was this 2–8–2, built in Germany in 1951, languishing in the shed at Huancayo.

December 1981

Huancavelica is eighty miles from Huancayo but it took the best part of the day for the mixed to get there. The train stopped everywhere and was full of people going to market with their produce and animals. The scenery is stunning. Never once does the line run at less than 10,000 ft above sea-level, and the Andes are a magnificent backdrop. To quote one writer, 'into those miles are packed all the requisites for a great mountain railway route with narrow gorges, swirling river torrents, tunnels and bridges, steep grades and rattling descents'. It was an exciting and exhilarating return journey, since like the loco, we stabled overnight in Huancavelica and returned on the next day's mixed.

The train pauses at a remote loop deep in the mountains.

December 1981

With the boiler-mounted bell clanging to warn of her approach, 107 pulls the stock of the daily mixed to Huancayo into Huancavelica station. Built by the British firm of Hunslet in 1936, she was an oil-fired 2–8–0.

This photograph is a personal favourite, partly because of the memories it revives, and partly because it shows steam going about its everyday business – not as a tourist attraction but doing a real job of work. The locals are paying not the slightest attention to the engine. They are more concerned with getting a seat.

December 1981

The large and the small. 309, a huge metre gauge 2–10–4, leaves Pinheirinho with a train of coal wagons bound for Capivari power station, Brazil. 488, an 0–6–0 tank, poses for the photographer at Temuco shed, Chile. Both were products of the Baldwin Locomotive Company, Philadelphia, USA. The former was constructed in 1940, the latter in 1907.

November and December 1981

Two curiosities: signals at Pua, Chile, and the waiting room at Chunca, Peru.

December 1981

North America

In a country which prides itself on industrial and technological innovation, it is inevitable that the USA was in the forefront of electrification and dieselization. Indeed, cynics have blamed the relentless elimination of steam worldwide on zealous American diesel salesmen! Fortunately, the USA and Canada were major exporters of steam locos, and as depicted in this book, their products survived into the 1980s in countries whose economies did not have the hard currency for wholesale 'modernization'.

Good though it is to see American engines in other parts of the world, one has to go to the USA for the authentic flavour of American steam railroads. It is a 'whole new ballgame' to the European eye. Much is strange: the appearance of locos and rolling stock, the method of operation, and the terminology. No prizes for knowing a 'Pacific' has a 4–6–2 wheel arrangement. But a 'Confederation'? (Answer: 4–8–4.)

Americans love their past and are aware of the importance railroads played in the expansion and development of their country. Museums and preserved railways can be found throughout the States.

Colorado has the Durango and Silverton Narrow Gauge RR, and the Cumbres and Toltec Scenic RR, two of the most spectacular lines. Both were once part of the 3 ft gauge Denver and Rio Grande system built in the late nineteenth century to tap the mineral wealth of the Rocky Mountains, south and west of Denver. Though today run primarily as tourist attractions, these lines are real railways with all the atmosphere of American steam.

And what scenery! The State of Colorado claims to have 1,000 peaks over 10,000 ft high. The line from Durango to Silverton runs 45 miles *through* the mountains, making use of the Animas River gorge. The Cumbres and Toltec Scenic RR goes *over* them, reaching a summit of 10,015 ft in the course of the 64 miles from Chama (New Mexico) to Antonito (Colorado).

To visit these railways is a must for the American steam buff. But don't just look. If you do, you'll be branded a rubber-necker! Ride the trains. Steep gradients, powerful engines and stunning scenery combine to provide an exciting railroad experience.

In the peak summer season, the Durango and Silverton Narrow Gauge RR runs four trains in each direction. American tourists must be up and about early because the first train leaves Durango at 7.30 a.m. An hour later it approaches Rockwood, having climbed 800 ft. There are 1,900 ft and two and a bit hours still to go before Silverton is reached.

June 1990

Like all the other locos on the line, 481 is a 2–8–2, or as the Americans say, a 'Mikado'. She is seen at exactly the same location as the previous photograph hauling the second departure from Durango.

June 1990

What in England is termed an unguarded level crossing is a common feature in the USA. 476 charges across Highway 550 at Hermosa with a train for Silverton.

June 1990

Circular wooden water tanks were a distinctive sight on American railroads in steam days. Sadly, the one at Hermosa is in poor condition and its role has been usurped by the undignified structure alongside. According to the plaque on the tank, the Rio Grande described itself as the 'scenic line of the world'.

June 1990

With scenery like this, the Rio Grande's claim was no idle boast. A train bound for Durango crosses the Animas River shortly after leaving Silverton. In early summer, there is still snow on the mountain tops.

June 1990

The same bridge from a different viewpoint.

June 1990

The engineer and conductor swap news at Durango.

June 1990

Sister locos 488 and 489 storm out of Chama on the Cumbres and Toltec Scenic RR. One could hear them a mile away before they burst into view. What a sight and sound!

June 1990

From Chama to the top of the Cumbres Pass, the railway climbs 2,100 ft in only 13½ miles. At one point, the line runs through a cleft in the mountains known as 'the Narrows', on a gradient of 1 in 25 (a 4% grade, in American jargon).

488 and 489 emerge from 'the Narrows'.

June 1990

If trains are double-headed, the leading engine is detached at Cumbres and sent back to Chama. There's no turntable, so the loco is turned on a 'Y'-shaped piece of track called, unsurprisingly, a wye. In years gone by, this was completely enclosed by a wooden snowshed. Only a part of the protection survives, but it is enough for Cumbres to claim the only covered wye still in use in the USA.

The previous day, 488 had hauled a special train chartered by a group of rail buffs, who had temporarily rechristened the railroad. I've no idea where the real 'Gadsden-Pacific' was, or if it ever existed.

June 1990

ZIMBABWE

In the 1980s, Zimbabwe witnessed a minor miracle in the history of steam. Prior to legal independence in 1980, the country was finding it difficult and expensive to obtain oil. As a consequence, dieselization of the country's 3 ft 6 in gauge network was halted and the decision taken to refurbish part of the railway's steam fleet. Resources were concentrated on the Garratts. Other 'conventional' locos were withdrawn from active service. The result was a railway system whose steam roster was uniquely completely Garratt, and with a few exceptions, the whole fleet was British built.

The railway authorities allowed one to ride in the cab of locos provided the necessary insurance indemnity had been signed in advance. This privilege permitted the ultimate steam experience. A Garratt in full cry is a magnificent sight. From the footplate, the sensation is awesome. Add to all of this the scenic attractions of the African bush and it is easy to see why Zimbabwe exerted a pull on railway enthusiasts in recent years. Natural wonders such as the Victoria Falls and the wildlife greatly added to the enjoyment.

At the end of the 1980s, steam activity was concentrated on three routes radiating from Bulawayo: north to Thomson Junction, Victoria Falls and Zambia; south to Plumtree (used by through traffic to and from South Africa); and the West Nicholson branch.

On the West Nicholson line, 612 pounds through the Mulungwane gorge at the head of a goods train. She has a 2–8–2 + 2–8–2 wheel arrangement.

July 1989

424, a 4–6–4 + 4–6–4 of 1951 vintage, climbs the grade near Syringa with a freight from Plumtree to Bulawayo.

July 1989

Much of the rail network is single track, which means trains have to make lengthy stops at crossing places. Using a car, the photographer has no difficulty chasing a train and photographing it in a number of different locations.

424 is seen again on the same train.

July 1989

The Garratts of Zimbabwe were of four wheel arrangements. Two have been noted. The third was 4–8–2 + 2–8–4.

733 takes water at the delightfully-named Figtree with a goods from Bulawayo to Plumtree.

July 1989

The daily all-stations passenger train from Plumtree to Bulawayo rolls into Marula.

July 1989

There was a once-a-week service from Bulawayo to Johannesburg. For the railway enthusiast, this was something of a collector's piece, for by the late 1980s there weren't many steam-hauled international passenger trains to be found anywhere in the world. The southbound working approaches Plumtree.

July 1989

There is one natural hazard to railway photography in the tropics. During the middle of the day, the sun is high in the sky, causing the wheels and motion of a steam engine to be in shadow. The best time for photography is therefore early morning or late afternoon when the low angle of the sun produces an even illumination.

On a cold winter's morning an hour after dawn, 415 strains to lift a heavy coal train around the horseshoe curve at Hwange.

July 1989

The line from Bulawayo to Victoria Falls is worked as two sections, the changeover point being Thomson Junction (TJ in local railway parlance) where connection is made with the Wankie Colliery private railway.

There are some fierce gradients north and south of TJ giving the Garratts the chance to show off their power. 381 pounds uphill near Zanguja with the 11.50 a.m. freight from TJ to Victoria Falls. The day after this photograph was taken, I rode in the cab of sister engine 377 on the very same working. Five hours after climbing on to the footplate at TJ sheds, I arrived elated at Victoria Falls station. It had been *the* most thrilling railway journey.

July 1989

A freight from TJ to Bulawayo passes a baobab tree near Lukosi.

July 1989

Perched on a hill, the Baobab Hotel at Hwange has a splendid view. Outside, one can relax with a cool beer and watch the trains for miles.

July 1989

Crocodile Bridge, near Mbalabala, on the West Nicholson branch.

July 1989

Early morning at Bulawayo shed. This photograph was carefully composed . . .

. . . but I had no idea how this one would turn out.

July 1989

Steam loco sheds are wonderfully atmospheric places, especially at first light . . .

. . . and towards dusk. These small Garratts had a 2–6–2 + 2–6–2 wheel arrangement, and were used on shunting duties at Bulawayo station and yards.

July 1989

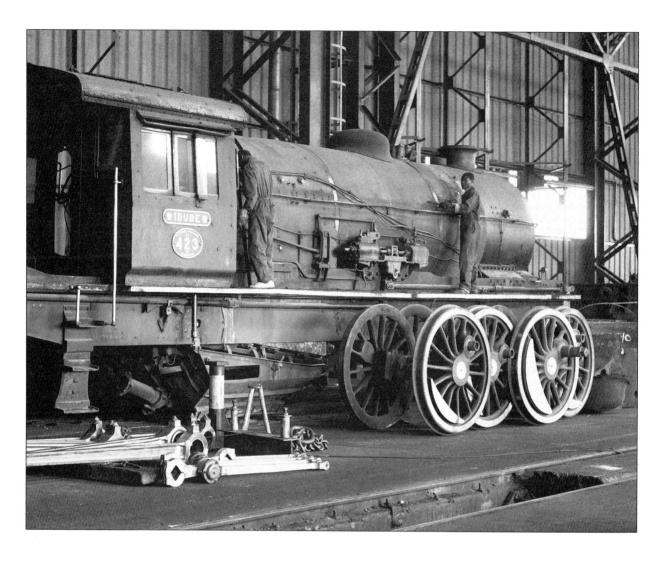

The rehabilitation of the Garratts was undertaken at the works of ZECO, a steel construction firm in Bulawayo.

At the time of rebuilding, some of the Garratts were given names of local origin. One class was named after birds and animals; another after rivers and regiments. *Idube* is the local name for zebra.

July 1989

The frames of another loco receive attention at ZECO. How heartening it was to see steam engines being given a new lease of life instead of being consigned to the scrap-heap.

July 1989

Wankie Colliery has its own private railway. No 1 was a 4–8–2 built by the North British
Locomotive Company in 1955.

July 1989

A train of empties *en route* from the exchange sidings at TJ to the colliery.

July 1989

Coal dust everywhere! There's nearly as much in the sky as on the ground, as two of the colliery's locos head a rake of empties.

July 1989

409 catches the last of the evening sun as she sits under the coaling plant at Thomson Junction shed.

July 1989

'When the trains stop, that will be the end' – Lenin

The last train of the day on the *Chemin de Fer de la Baie de Somme*, France.

May 1988